SANKOFA
BLACK HERITAGE COLLECTION

TRADITIONS AND CELEBRATIONS

NICOLE RICKETTS

SERIES EDITOR • TOM HENDERSON

www.rubiconpublishing.com

Associate Publisher: Amy Land
Project Editor: Jessica Rose
Editor: Mariana Aldave
Creative Director: Jennifer Drew
Lead Designer: Sherwin Flores
Graphic Designers: Robin Forsyth, Jen Harvey, Robin Lindner, Jason Mitchell

Every reasonable effort has been made to trace the owners of copyrighted
material and to make due acknowledgement. Any errors or omissions
drawn to our attention will be gladly rectified in future editions.

16 17 18 19 20   6 5 4 3 2

ISBN: 978-1-77058-825-7

We acknowledge the financial support of the Government of Canada through
the Canada Book Fund for our publishing activities.

Printed in Canada

CONTENTS

TRADITIONS AND CELEBRATIONS

Each country in Africa has unique traditions and celebrations. However, all countries celebrate with food, music, and a deep sense of community.

Traditions and celebrations in African culture do not take place only in Africa. They also take place in the Caribbean, Canada, and all over the world. By sharing their traditions and celebrations with the world, people of African descent let everyone know who they are.

In this book, you'll read about how people of African descent share their traditions and celebrations of African culture with the rest of the world.

How do our traditions and celebrations define who we are?

Let's CELEBRATE

THINK ABOUT IT

Celebrations are important traditions in a community. They mark special events and remind others of people's accomplishments. What celebrations are unique in your community?

THE CULTURE AND TRADITIONS of people of African descent are celebrated around the world. Parades, art, sports, and food are just a few ways people of African descent celebrate their culture. This timeline will tell you about some of these events.

JANUARY

Martin Luther King Jr. Day

The Africentric Alternative School in Toronto celebrates Martin Luther King Jr. Day.

Every year, on the third Monday in January, people celebrate the life and achievements of Martin Luther King Jr. King was a leader in the American Civil Rights Movement. Martin Luther King Jr. Day is a public holiday in the United States. On this day, people attend parades and do volunteer work.

In their 2014 celebration of Martin Luther King Jr. Day, students from the Africentric Alternative School in Toronto, Ontario, sang, danced, and played the drums to honour the vision, courage, and contributions of King. A student in grade 6 delivered King's famous "I Have a Dream" speech, which was given at the historic March on Washington in 1963.

In 2014, NASA celebrated Martin Luther King Jr. Day by tweeting an image of King's place of birth, Atlanta, Georgia.

FEBRUARY

Black History Month

Black History Month is a time to learn about the experiences, contributions, and accomplishments of men and women of African descent. It is celebrated in the United States, Canada, and the United Kingdom.

Each year, Canada Post releases stamps to commemorate Black History Month. The 2014 stamps featured two places of historic significance to African Canadians: Hogan's Alley, in Vancouver, British Columbia, and Africville, in Halifax, Nova Scotia.

MARCH

Harriet Tubman Day

On 10 March, Harriet Tubman Day celebrates the most famous conductor of the Underground Railroad. Tubman escaped from slavery in Maryland, United States, in 1849. She travelled to St. Catharines, Ontario. After her own escape, she helped hundreds of others escape to Canada. "I never ran my train off the track, and I never lost a passenger," she said.

March 2013 marked 100 years since Tubman's death. The city of St. Catharines celebrated her life and work at the church she attended there, Salem Chapel. A local choir performed and a ceremony was held.

APRIL

Harare International Festival of the Arts (HIFA)

The Harare International Festival of the Arts (HIFA) is a six-day event that takes place in Zimbabwe. It is a celebration of local, regional, and international art and culture. There are performances of all kinds, including music, theatre, circus, and spoken word.

Youth have a dedicated area at HIFA called the Simba Youth Zone. This area offers performances and workshops on drumming, storytelling, and spoken word.

Grammy-winning singer Dobet Gnahoré from the Republic of Côte d'Ivoire performs at HIFA in 2014.

MAY

Africa Day

On 25 May, Africa Day celebrates the founding of the Organisation of African Unity (OAU) in 1963. The organization was created to promote unity among African countries. Today, the OAU is known as the African Union. On Africa Day, many countries hold gala dinners and artistic performances. They also hold festivals and sporting events that celebrate Africa.

Dancers perform during the 2013 celebrations of Africa Day in Addis Ababa, Ethiopia.

JUNE

Schoolchildren dance at a Juneteenth celebration in San Diego, California.

Juneteenth

Juneteenth celebrates the end of slavery in the United States. It marks 19 June 1865, the day when enslaved Africans in Texas heard that they were finally free.

Juneteenth celebrations are held in most American states and in many countries around the world. The Essence International School in Kaduna, Nigeria, posted this ad in 2010: "We will celebrate Juneteenth with Afro-American jazz music, popular music, and African drumming. The entertainment will include a mock wedding — jumping over the broomstick as in the olden days, poetry recitations, and singing."

enslaved: *being captured and sold into slavery*

JULY

Afrofest

This annual African music festival started in Toronto in 1989. Afrofest celebrates the diversity of Africa as a continent. It showcases African music and culture. The festival features authentic foods such as fried plantain, fresh coconut juice, cassava, and catfish in a banana leaf. Vendors sell traditional clothes, jewellery, arts, and crafts.

Dancers from the Southern Volta Association of Canada, a Ghanaian cultural group, perform at the 2013 Afrofest at Queen's Park, Toronto.

AUGUST

Performance during Homowo in Accra, Ghana

Homowo

"Let's mock the past hunger season and welcome the new period of plenty." This is the meaning of the Homowo festival. The Ga people of Ghana once suffered a severe famine due to lack of rain. They worked hard on their land and were rewarded with a great harvest. The festival is a reminder of that difficult time and a celebration of the victory over hunger. The festival starts in May with the planting of crops. There is then a period of silence to help the crops bear fruit. Celebrations take place through August and September, which is the end of the harvest season. People march down the streets dancing, beating drums, and chanting. People hug and wish one another a good year. On the last day, people eat a special meal of *kpokpoi* (a kind of flour and oil mixture) and palm nut soup.

famine: *severe shortage of food*

SEPTEMBER

Heritage Day

On 24 September, South Africa celebrates its different cultures, traditions, and languages. The National Indigenous Games are held as a buildup to Heritage Day celebrations. The event features traditional games like *dibeke* (a running ball game), *intonga* (a stick-fighting martial art), and *jukskei* (a kind of horseshoe-pitching game). Nelisiwe Moerane, a member of the province of Gauteng's Sport, Arts, Culture and Recreation Committee, said: "The purpose of these games is to make the youth not to forget about the sporting activities that their ancestors played and to further instill pride for these games. This is a … program that will help … to promote our heritage as a province and country at large."

In jukskei, players throw a skey (a kind of bar) to try to get close to a peg to score points.

OCTOBER

Festival Kreol

People celebrate at the Festival Kreol in Victoria, Seychelles.

Festival Kreol runs for six days on the Seychelles islands. It is a celebration of the islands' Creole identity and culture. "Creole" refers to a person of mixed European and African descent. It also refers to a language formed from the contact of a European language (such as English, French, or Spanish) with a local language.

The people in Seychelles are proud to promote their Creole language and culture. They do so through music, dance, art, and traditional food. Performing artists and painters from other Creole-speaking countries, including Haiti and Martinique, participate in the celebrations as well.

NOVEMBER

Remembrance Day

On 11 November at 11 a.m., Canadians pay tribute to soldiers who served Canada in past wars. It is also a day to honour all those who sacrificed their lives in military service. Many African Canadians volunteered to serve the country in World War I. Black men and women were not allowed to participate in the war effort at the time. However, men were later assigned non-combatant support roles. Black women worked as nurses at home and worked in ammunition factories. World War II saw African Canadian soldiers playing larger roles at home and on the battlefields. Today, there is much more diversity in the Canadian Forces.

DECEMBER

Kwanzaa

Kinara

Kwanzaa is a holiday that takes place between 26 December and 1 January. It celebrates Black identity, encourages unity, and preserves African culture. Dr. Maulana Karenga created Kwanzaa in 1966.

Kwanzaa is based upon harvest traditions and values found throughout Africa. A symbol of Kwanzaa is a candle holder called the *kinara*. It has seven holes for candles. Each candle represents a day of celebration.

Kwanzaa includes a time for reflection, a time for artistic performances, and a time to enjoy traditional foods, such as *benne* (sesame seed) cakes. Sesame seeds are traditionally eaten for good luck.

CONNECT IT

What special event or person do you think should be celebrated in your community? Write a short proposal for a special celebration in your community.

CELEBRATE EVERY OCCASION

THINK ABOUT IT

Rites of passage mark important transitions in the lives of people of African descent. In a small group, share a memory about an important celebration in someone's life.

NOT ALL FAMILIES, communities, or countries celebrate the same events. Even if they do celebrate the same event, they might do so in different ways. Read these short reports about how some communities celebrate important events in a person's life.

BIRTH

Egyptians welcome a baby with a great celebration called *sebou*. It happens one week after the baby's birth. The word "sebou" means "seventh day." Candles, flowers, and fruit are used in this celebration. These are symbols of growth and life. As part of the traditional celebration, the mother jumps over the baby seven times.

A big part of sebou is having friends and family over. Visitors bring gifts for the baby, such as gold bracelets for girls and amulets for boys. The new mother might get a gift, too. As for food, some of the traditional elements include *aqiqah* (lamb meat) and *moghat* (a special hot beverage).

A baby sleeps through his sebou celebration.

BIRTHDAYS

Flour is an important part of birthdays in Jamaica. It's not used only in cake. A Jamaican tradition is to throw some flour over the head of the person who is having a birthday. The flour throwing takes place when the person is least expecting it. It might not be very amusing to some people, but is much better than being egged (another Jamaican birthday tradition).

COMING OF AGE

Coming of age is an important milestone in any culture. It is the time when children become adults. In many African communities, young adults are considered old enough to learn the laws, customs, and traditions of their people. They are also permitted to marry and start families of their own.

Young Kota men from the Republic of the Congo celebrate coming of age by painting themselves blue. For the Kota, blue is the colour of death. This tradition symbolizes that the boy in the man has died.

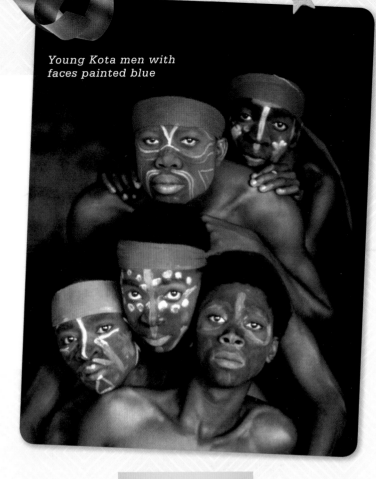

Young Kota men with faces painted blue

DEATH

A funeral in Ghana is a very special celebration. People present gifts, such as pieces of cloth, drinks, and money, before the burial. These items are placed in the coffin. They are meant to assist in the dead person's journey to the spiritual world. Families spend a lot of money on a funeral, which includes music and dancing.

A fantasy coffin in a shape of a fish is displayed in an exhibition. People from Ghana often create fantasy coffins that represent the profession or the interests of the person who has died.

CONNECT IT

Choose one of the celebrations in this selection, and do some additional research to see how the tradition is celebrated in another culture. Write a short report of your findings. As an alternative, you may research a celebration that has not been shared. Choose a culture and write a short report on how that tradition is celebrated in the culture you chose.

GULLAH

KEEPING A CULTURE ALIVE

THINK ABOUT IT

Imagine that you live in a community far away from other people. What might be the benefits of this? What might be the disadvantages?

THE GULLAH, OR GEECHEE, people are originally from countries in West Africa. In the 1700s, many were taken as enslaved Africans to work on plantations on the Sea Islands. The Sea Islands are on the southeast coast of the United States. They were not easy to access at the time. Plantation owners did not spend a lot of time on the islands. The Gullah were left on their own for long periods of time. This isolation helped them keep their African culture, traditions, and celebrations alive. Learn more in these fact cards.

LANGUAGE

THEN: African American linguist Lorenzo Dow Turner first recorded Gullah speakers in the 1930s. He recorded their unique language, which mixes African and English words and structures. Gullah is mostly an oral language. However, some people have tried to preserve it in written form. It uses short, loosely connected sentences. Gullah speakers express different meanings by varying tone and pitch. They also use body language.

Lorenzo Dow Turner

NOW: Queen Quet is the head of state for the Gullah/Geechee Nation. She has spent most of her life preserving the heritage of the Gullah people and their language. Queen Quet is engaging younger generations by communicating in Gullah on social media sites. Through Twitter and Facebook, the younger generation is gaining a greater appreciation of the legacy they have inherited.

linguist: *person who studies language and its structure*

head of state: *chief public representative of a nation*

Queen Quet

STORYTELLING

THEN: Enslaved Africans used stories as forms of expression. The experiences they had on plantations, mixed with the customs that they brought with them from Africa, gave life to many folk tales and stories.

Brer Rabbit

One character in Gullah stories is Brer Rabbit. Brer Rabbit is a trickster who often outwits his opponents. However, his dishonest tactics sometimes get him into serious trouble.

NOW: Many Gullah storytellers carry on the storytelling tradition. Anita Singleton-Prather and Carolyn "Jabulile" White entertain and educate audiences of all ages.

Anita Singleton-Prather

MUSIC

THEN: When enslaved, the Gullah were not allowed to use drums. They made music using mortars and pestles instead. When these were no longer allowed, they used sticks, along with their hands, feet, voices, and whole bodies.

Stick pounding is part of the Gullah tradition. Enslaved Africans turned their praise houses into big drums by pounding a broom or stick on the floor. They also did a dance called a ring shout. Dancers moved counter-clockwise (never crossing their feet) while clapping their hands (always above the waist).

The Old Plantation, *1800*

NOW: Musician Melanie DeMore carries on the Gullah art of stick pounding. In her workshops, a combination of foot stomping, hand clapping, stick pounding, and singing helps participants learn about the Gullah/Geechee culture.

praise houses: *small shacks used for gatherings*

Melanie DeMore

ARTS AND CRAFTS

THEN: Most Gullah arts and crafts traditions originated in West Africa. Baskets were made to make daily work easier. In the United States, baskets were used to collect cotton and rice. The most common materials used to make baskets were sweetgrass, palmetto leaves, and longleaf pine needles. Gullah fishers knitted their own fishing nets with a needle, which was often made of palmetto wood.

Strip quilting was also part of the Gullah tradition. Quilts told family and personal stories from the past. Quilts were made from strips of cloth. They were often modelled on the quilts made on looms in many parts of West Africa.

A Gullah woman weaves a basket out of sweetgrass.

NOW: Gullah men continue their woodcarving tradition. Some carve grave monuments, human figures, and walking sticks. Women still make baskets, which are now more of pieces of art than practical tools. Visitors in South Carolina can watch women make baskets at the Charleston City Market or on the Sea Islands.

CONNECT IT

The Gullah have worked hard to keep their traditions alive. They are proud to show them to the world. Why do you think it is worth working hard to keep traditions alive? What family or cultural tradition would you fight to keep alive?

THE DISTANT TALKING DRUM

■ BY ISAAC OLALEYE

THINK ABOUT IT

Use the title of this poem and the images found on this page to predict what "The Distant Talking Drum" might be about. Share your ideas with a classmate.

ABOUT THE POET

Isaac Olaleye was born in Nigeria and raised in a very large family. He had 13 brothers and sisters. When Olaleye was very young, he took jobs to pay for his education in England. He studied law and economics. However, once he settled in the United States, he became a full-time writer. He adapts his childhood memories and experiences from Nigeria into stories for young readers.

IN AFRICAN CULTURES, drums could be beating for many reasons. There could be an announcement, a gathering, or maybe a celebration. In African tradition, drums are both a musical instrument and a method of communication.

One type of drum used to communicate is a talking drum. Just like telephones, talking drums are used to share messages over far distances. Talking drums are traditionally carved from wood and covered with the hide of an animal. The drummer places the talking drum under his or her arm. One hand is used to beat the hide with a stick to create a sound. At the same time, the drummer squeezes the strings around the drum to adjust the tone and mimic a "talking" sound.

Musicians and storytellers use the talking drums in traditional celebrations. Read this poem to learn more about drumming in rural Nigeria.

From deep in the rainforest
The sound of a distant talking drum I hear —
Far away, far away.
For me it calls.
Clearly it calls
For me to dance,
For men to dance,
For women to dance,
For children to dance.

And the sound of the distant drum
Echoes through the rainforest.
The distant talking drum
Is calling across the mighty rainforest
For me to come,
For me to dance.
Now the sound of sweet songs
I hear.
Beautifully they flow!

And the distant talking drum
Is still calling
Far away, far away.
Clearly it calls
For me to come,
For me to dance.
So across the rainforest,
The wide, wild, and wonderful rainforest,
I go!

CONNECT IT

In a small group, create a soundscape
using this poem. The soundscape
should consider not only the music of
the drum, but also the rainforest and
emotions in the poem. Share your
soundscape with another group.

MAKE YOUR OWN
TOY

THINK ABOUT IT

Think about a favourite toy you had or made when you were younger. Tell a partner why this toy is memorable.

MATERIALS:

- 10 to 15 corn husks
- scissors

WHAT'S YOUR FAVOURITE way to pass the time? You might say listening to music, playing video games, or surfing the Internet. But what would you do if you didn't have access to batteries or electricity?

In the past, people had to make their own toys using natural materials, such as wood or corn husks, or found objects. One of the toys people made was a corn husk doll. Enslaved Africans who lived on plantations in the United States and First Nations peoples of the Eastern Woodlands in Canada made corn husk dolls.

Follow these step-by-step instructions to make your own corn husk doll.

Step 1

Take six corn husks and tie them together, about 8 cm from the narrow end. Use a thin strip torn from a corn husk.

Step 2

Head: Take the corn husks above the knot. Roll them into a ball until they touch the knot. Then, take each corn husk from the bottom section and fold it up over the ball and back down the other side. Cover the ball completely.

Step 3

Neck: Tie another strip of corn husk under the head to form the neck.

Step 4

Arms: Cut a husk lengthwise into three strips. Tie them together about 2 cm from one end. Use another corn husk strip [to tie them together].

Step 5

Braid the husks. Tie the bottom, leaving about 2 cm. Trim the ends of each side to form a hand.

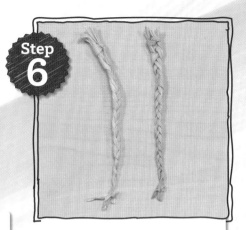

Step 6

Legs: Repeat steps 4 and 5 two times to make two legs.

Step 7

Lift up the upper layer of corn husks and place the centre of the braid for the arms near the head.

Step 8

Tummy: Roll a corn husk into a ball.

Step 9

Place the ball on top of the arms to make the doll's tummy.

Step 10

Place the braids for the legs under the tummy. Bring the corn husks back down to cover them.

Step 11

Waist: Take another strip of corn husk. Tie [it] tightly under the tummy to make the waist. To finish, trim the skirt to the length you want. Cut vertical slits in the skirt so that it will flare out.

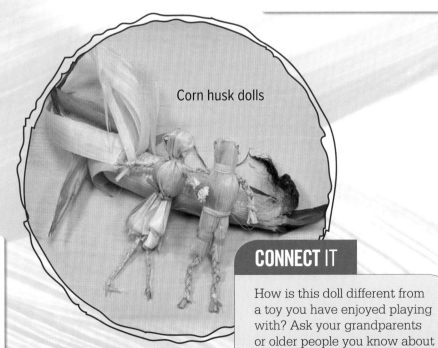

Corn husk dolls

CONNECT IT

How is this doll different from a toy you have enjoyed playing with? Ask your grandparents or older people you know about the toys they enjoyed when they were young. Share your stories in a group.

19

Nsue and the Honeyguide

RETOLD BY SHARON HOWARD

THINK ABOUT IT

In a small group, talk about the different roles taken by members of your family when preparing a meal. What is your role? How much do you enjoy it? Would you rather have a different role?

"NSUE AND THE HONEYGUIDE" is a short story of the San people, the first peoples of southern Africa. They are hunter-gatherers.

The story focuses on the celebration of the Festival of the New Moon. The story also mentions other traditions such as hunting, storytelling, and naming.

In this story, you'll see how celebrations strengthen traditions in communities and families.

Silently, he crept through jagged thorn bushes. Bare feet moved swiftly over hot, arid soil to the edge of a water hole where the kudu was drinking. The great animal suddenly looked up, spiral horns curving sharply into the endless African sky. Nsue (Neh-SOO-ee) did not reach for his pouch of poisoned arrows. He had no heart for killing. This would not be the day he would change his childish boyhood name.

arid: *very dry*
kudu: *type of African antelope*

Nsue left the salt pan and climbed the barren hillside to the cool twilight of the rock caves. Tonight would be the Festival of the New Moon, and Nsue had nothing to contribute to the feast. His sister, Nandi, had found four plump tsamma melons to share.

Nsue lay on his back and studied the ancient paintings that lined the rock walls. They reminded him of the many stories that Gao, the Old One, told about the San people of long ago. In this harsh desert climate, everyone must hunt for food to survive. Gao's stories honoured the brave hunters. Nsue wanted to hide in the caves until the stories were over. It was there that his father found him.

Nsue's father knew the reason for the boy's unhappiness. He had

Why do you think Nsue is upset?

often heard the older boys teasing his son about his name. Nsue means "ostrich egg." He was given this name because when he was a baby in a sling on his mother's back, his shiny oval head looked just like an ostrich egg gleaming in the sun.

"I will never be a skilled hunter like you, Father. I do not wish to kill the beautiful animals of our desert."

"Nsue is a fine name," his father said. "Ostrich eggs are of great value to our people. One egg can feed 12 hungry men. The empty shells are used to carry and store water. Even the broken pieces become tools or jewellery. Be proud of your name!"

Nsue turned his head away. "It is the name of a child, not a hunter," he cried. "I will never be a skilled hunter like you, Father. I do not wish to kill the beautiful animals of our desert."

Nsue's father squatted on his heels and surveyed the vast Kalahari beyond. "The spirit gods did not intend for all men to be hunters,"

Kalahari is the name of a desert in southern Africa. Some San people still live in parts of this desert.

he said softly. "Some men tell stories around the cooking fires. Others paint our history on the walls of the rock caves. Men like Nxou are keepers of water. Without water, even the bravest hunters would soon die."

---

salt pan: *natural depression in the ground where salt water gathers, evaporates, and then leaves a deposit of salt*

tsamma melons: *melons that grow in the wild in Africa*

Despite his anxiety, Nsue had to smile as he thought of skinny Nxou pressing a dry reed through the sand in just the right place, drawing water to fill 15 ostrich eggs for tonight's celebration. "I will find something to share at the Festival of the New Moon," Nsue promised as he left the cave and walked into the shimmering heat.

In time, Nsue grew tired and stopped to rest in the shade of a thornbush. At first, he thought the wind was playing tricks on his ears, but there it was again: "Nta-nta-nta-nteee!"

When he heard the excited cry of the honeyguide bird, Nsue leaped up and began to answer with the grunts and growls of the honey badger. As he ran along, he remembered the stories of Gao, who told of the bird who seeks out other creatures to invade the combs of honeybees.

Nsue ran like the desert wind, and eventually the honeyguide led him to the base of a baobab tree, standing like a lonely giant against the setting sun. The hollow tree revealed an opening, with bees buzzing angrily around the excited bird.

Nsue quickly tore a piece of fibrous bark from the case of the tree and began to climb. Without hesitation, he reached into the hollow centre and dipped his scoop into a great comb of golden honey. He returned to the ground so quickly that only a few bees were able to avenge the intrusion with angry stings.

Although Nsue was in a hurry, he remembered Gao's words: "If you do not leave a portion of the comb for the honeyguide who brought you to this golden treasure, the next time it will lead you to a hungry lion instead of thick, sweet honey."

> Both the honeyguide bird and the honey badger feed on honeybee combs. The honeyguide bird can easily locate the combs, but it can't always reach the wax and bee larvae it feeds on. The badger can easily open the combs, but it can't always find them without help. Some say the bird guides the badger to the combs with loud cries and by flying ahead. The badger uses its claws to get all the bee larvae and honey it wants, and the bird feeds on the remains.

> This is the third time Nsue thinks about Gao. How important do you think Gao's role in the community is?

It was dark when Nsue returned, and the Dance of the New Moon had already begun. His heart sang more loudly than the beautiful voices of the children. His face and arms were swollen from bee stings, but his lopsided grin was full of pride as he stepped forward and offered to share his golden prize.

As the music ended, his father announced, "From this day forward, my son shall be known to all as Ratel, the fierce and clever honey badger."

◀ What are some of the ways that the Festival of the New Moon celebration has changed Nsue?

CONNECT IT

Choose one character in this story. In role as the character you chose, write a journal entry that summarizes what happened in this story. Share your story in a small group. How is your story different from others written by the people in your group?

TELL ME A Story

THINK ABOUT IT

Think about the last time someone told you a story. Was the story read from a book? Was the story told from memory? Which do you prefer?

THESE SHORT PROFILES feature some of the greatest storytellers of African descent. These storytellers have hooked audiences all over the world.

MISS LOU
(1919–2006)

The Honourable Louise Bennett-Coverley was mostly known as "Miss Lou." She was born in Jamaica, but lived for many years in Canada. Miss Lou was a traditional storyteller, university lecturer, poet, and activist. She was passionate about Jamaican culture. Most of her stories and poems came from her love of Jamaica's rich cultural heritage. She wrote in Jamaican patois.

How It All Started:

"As you see, I like to tell stories. *Suh mi use to do, yuh know. An' mi use to try out on de people in de sewing room same way, yuh know. Go een man, and tell dem story and ting.* And I found that I had the gift of laughter. Anyhow, I used to go and try out my little things, and tell them jokes, and tell them stories."

– MISS LOU

This is written in patois. In standard English, it means "So I used to do so, you know. And I used to try them out on the people in [my mom's] sewing room, you know. People come in and I tell them stories and things."

Carol Adler and Edna Manley listen to Miss Lou's retelling of Jamaican folk stories.

CHINUA ACHEBE

(1930–2013)

Chinua Achebe was born in Eastern Nigeria. His given name was Albert Chinualumogu Achebe. Growing up in Ogidi, Nigeria, Achebe began to learn English at the age of eight. He was educated in English and wrote his novels in English. However, he felt it was important to support Igbo, his mother tongue.

Achebe was a novelist, poet, professor, and critic. His novels tell stories from an African point of view. Achebe's first novel, *Things Fall Apart*, talks about the difference in values between White people and people of African descent.

Chike and the River was Achebe's first novel for children. It is a tale of bravery and growth.

critic: *person who writes reviews, in this case, of literary works*

About Storytelling:

"If you don't like someone's story, write your own."

"It is the storyteller who makes us what we are, who creates history. The storyteller creates the memory that the survivors must have — otherwise their surviving would have no meaning."

"There is no story that is not true."
(said by Uchendu, a character in *Things Fall Apart*)

— CHINUA ACHEBE

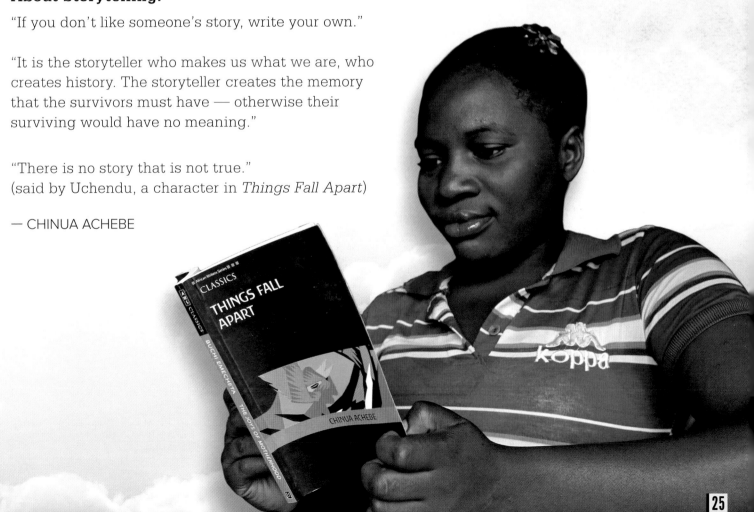

RICHARDO KEENS-DOUGLAS

(b. 1953)

Richardo Keens-Douglas was born on the Caribbean island of Grenada. He moved to Canada as a teenager. He began his career as an actor. He has appeared in films and on the stage, including at Canada's Stratford Festival. He is also a trained dancer in Afro-Caribbean jazz.

His love of literature and writing inspired him to write stories. His books for young children explore the African Caribbean experience and celebrate family. He shares his stories during school workshops, encouraging listeners to use their imagination. One of his books, *The Nutmeg Princess*, has been turned into an award-winning stage play.

About the Power of Storytelling:

"I had an incredible mom and dad. I remember growing up, we would be sitting on the veranda in a full moonlight … and my dad would say: 'OK. I remember when …' The moment he said that you knew it was storytime. It was part of the culture. It was part of the family … My mom was an incredible storyteller. … Monday night was my mom and dad's movie night. … And on Tuesday night, … my mom would sit on the bed, she would get all the kids around her, and she would tell us a story of the movie she saw the night before. That's to tell you how powerful storytelling was."

> How do you think these experiences as a young boy helped Keens-Douglas in his storytelling career?

– RICHARDO KEENS-DOUGLAS

THE NUTMEG PRINCESS

written by Richardo Keens-Douglas
illustrated by Annouchka Galouchko

New Edition

The Nutmeg Princess by Richardo Keens-Douglas

ITAH SADU
(b. 1961)

Itah Sadu was born in Canada, but she was raised in Barbados. She eventually returned to Canada, where she became an author of children's books and celebrated storyteller.

Sadu uses storytelling to celebrate culture, explain history, and talk about everyday issues. Not only do her stories entertain audiences, but they also start conversations. For example, in *Christopher Changes His Name*, Sadu gives children a chance to talk about how special names can be.

A Review of *Christopher Changes His Name*:

"It is not hard to imagine that all kids have had an 'I hate my name!' thought at least once in their lives. So it is quite [understandable] that children will be able to relate to, and laugh at, this young boy who hates his boring, commonplace name with a passion.

In this entertaining little book, readers meet Christopher, who despises his name and decides to change a mundane name into an extraordinary name, one that is uniquely memorable. He tries a few: 'Tiger,' after a famous Trinidadian strong man; 'The Real McCoy,' even '23,' after his favourite basketball player. All his friends thought these were great names and even wanted to change their own. His teacher and his mom thought it was all a bit foolish. One day, however, Christopher/Tiger/Real McCoy/23 learns that using your own name can be very important in dealing with real-life problems."

— THE CANADIAN REVIEW OF MATERIALS,
  © THE MANITOBA LIBRARY ASSOCIATION

> Which part of this review makes you want to read the book?

Itah Sadu at a book signing

CONNECT IT

Everybody has a story to tell. Make up your own story and share it with a family member or friend. Before you do so, think about what makes a good storyteller.

CRABS FOR DINNER

THINK ABOUT IT

Does your family have a tradition that involves food? If so, why is this tradition important to your family? If your family has other traditions, why are those traditions important?

ABOUT THE AUTHOR

Adwoa Badoe was born and raised in Ghana, where she worked as a doctor. When she moved to Canada, Badoe had difficulty finding a job in the medical field. This was upsetting, but it did not stop her from fulfilling other dreams. Badoe became a published author, storyteller, and African dance instructor. She loves sharing her love for Africa and its traditions with readers and students.

BY ADWOA BADOE

MOVING TO A faraway country can be difficult. Many people carry on traditions that remind them of home. However, children born or raised in Canada might not understand their parents' or grandparents' traditions from home. Read what happens when traditional food prepared by a Ghanaian grandmother lands on the plates of two children raised in Canada.

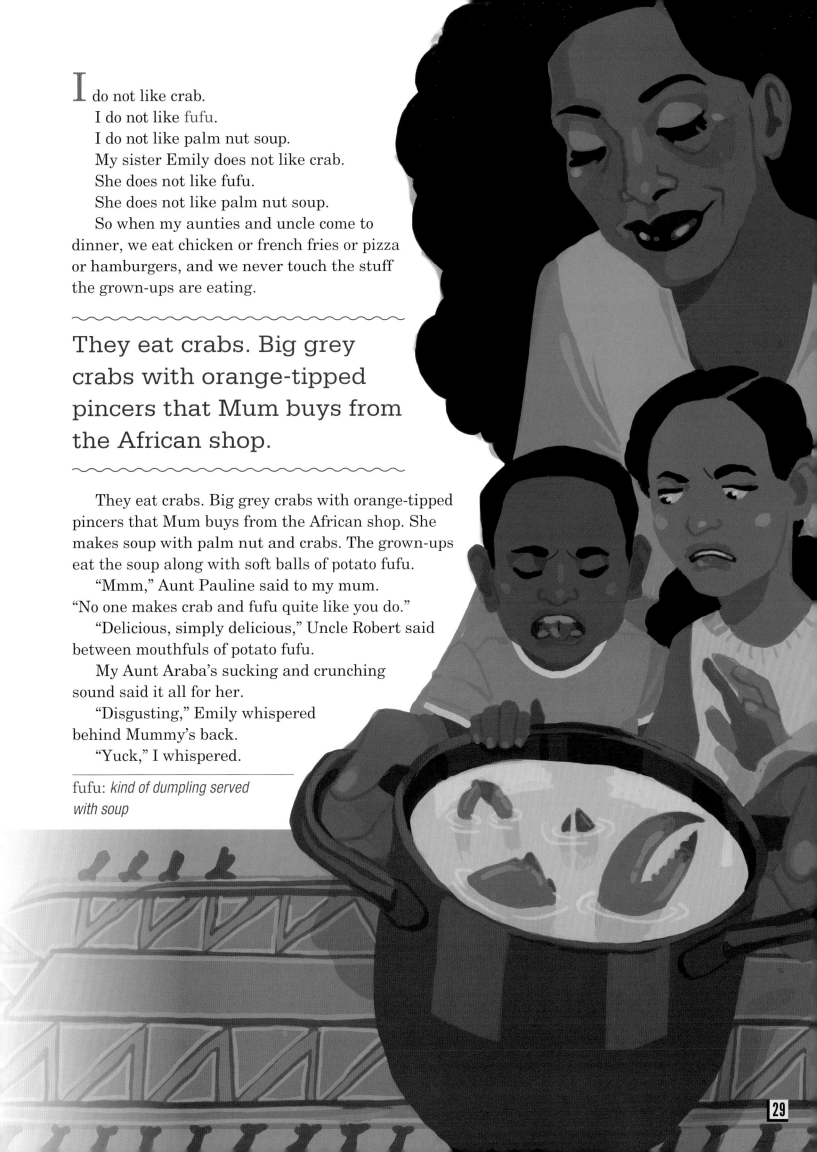

I do not like crab.

I do not like fufu.

I do not like palm nut soup.

My sister Emily does not like crab.

She does not like fufu.

She does not like palm nut soup.

So when my aunties and uncle come to dinner, we eat chicken or french fries or pizza or hamburgers, and we never touch the stuff the grown-ups are eating.

They eat crabs. Big grey crabs with orange-tipped pincers that Mum buys from the African shop.

They eat crabs. Big grey crabs with orange-tipped pincers that Mum buys from the African shop. She makes soup with palm nut and crabs. The grown-ups eat the soup along with soft balls of potato fufu.

"Mmm," Aunt Pauline said to my mum. "No one makes crab and fufu quite like you do."

"Delicious, simply delicious," Uncle Robert said between mouthfuls of potato fufu.

My Aunt Araba's sucking and crunching sound said it all for her.

"Disgusting," Emily whispered behind Mummy's back.

"Yuck," I whispered.

fufu: *kind of dumpling served with soup*

One summer, my grandmother came for a visit all the way from Africa.

"Ghana," she said. "That's where I come from."

She brought us funny-looking clothes, the kind they wear in Ghana. I had a smock made of a rough cotton fabric with stripes of bright colours woven into it.

It was long and loose, almost like a dress. Grandma said it was meant to be worn over a pair of trousers.

"I'm never going to wear those," I said to my mum.

Grandma had lots of stories to tell. Stories her grandmother told her when she was young.

But Emily wore hers, a colourful batik dress with embroidery around the neck.

She looked so pretty that I decided to wear my smock. When I did, I thought I looked "cool." Especially when I wore the striped cotton cap that came with the smock.

Grandma had lots of stories to tell. Stories her grandmother told her when she was young. I liked the ones about a cunning "Spider man" who got in and out of all kinds of trouble.

She always ended in a funny way, saying, "This story of mine, whether good or bad, may pass away, or come to stay. It is your turn to tell your story."

So, we took our turn and told her stories. And she liked them just as much as we liked hers.

smock: *light, loose dress*
batik: *cloth that has been dyed*

A week before she left for Ghana, she invited my aunts and uncle to dinner.

"She's going to make soup and yucky crab," Emily said. "I'll bet she makes a lot of it. But I won't even take a bite."

She did make the soup, only she put in okra, too.

"That's going to make it slimy," I said.

"Double yuck," said Emily.

But dinner got cooked and dinner was served and grace was said.

Emily and I were eating hot dogs and the grown-ups were eating slime.

Uncle Robert rolled his eyes upward.

"Mmm," he said. "Exquisite!"

I had never heard him use that word for Mum's soup.

"My word," Aunt Pauline said. "I had almost forgotten the original taste."

My mum simply said, "Delicious."

Even Aunt Araba paused from the sucking and crunching to say one word, "Authentic!"

I noticed that Grandma's soup smelled really good, much better than Mum's soup. Suddenly, I wanted to taste just a little bit of the fufu with crab and soup.

"Can I have a little, please?" I heard Emily ask.

"Why, of course!" Grandma replied.

If Emily doesn't die, I'll have some, I thought. Emily took a bite and didn't die.

Instead, she took another bite.

"And how about you?" said Grandma.

"Yes, please," I said.

It tasted different, not like the soups I knew. It was spicy and hot and really good. It was thick and smooth, and I thought I could taste the flavour of ginger.

I broke off a tiny piece of crab and sucked it just like Mummy did. It was all soft inside. Then, I crunched on it, really hard, just as my Aunt Araba did.

Then, I ate a whole bowl of fufu and soup and a huge piece of crab.

When I was done, I rolled my eyes up to the sky and said aloud, "Exquisite!"

I am not even sure what that means, but probably it is a way of saying that sometimes grandmothers cook better than mothers.

CONNECT IT

Imagine you are one of the children in this story. In role, write a letter to Grandma. Write about how your experience eating Grandma's traditional food and wearing traditional African clothing changed what you felt about traditions.

The FLAVOURS of AFRICA

THINK ABOUT IT

With a partner, discuss how food might be a way for people to express their culture.

AFRICAN CUISINE IS rich in variety, flavours, and aromas. Food etiquette differs among countries, too. Read these fact cards about just a few African food traditions.

Food etiquette: *table manners*

ETHIOPIA

Typical Dish: The most popular traditional food in Ethiopia is *wat*. Wat is a stew prepared with beef, chicken, or lamb, a variety of vegetables, and spices. It is served on *injera*, a type of flatbread.

Food Etiquette: Traditionally, Ethiopians don't use utensils when eating. They take a piece of injera in their right hand to scoop up the food.

Drink Up! Ethiopia is well known for its coffee. Every meal ends with a coffee ceremony, which involves roasting, grinding, and brewing coffee in a traditional clay pot called a *jebena*. The host pours coffee for all guests without stopping between cups.

Ethiopians in Canada: "We value difference and we live together under one flag. We have more than 80 dialects and three major religions, and yet we've managed to live without interethnic and religious conflict. We respect and honour each other."

— Muluken Muchie, owner and editor of the Toronto-based Ethiopian newspaper *Hawarya*

Wat with injera

A woman prepares a coffee ceremony while a man plays a masenqo (a traditional Ethiopian instrument).

MOROCCO

Tajine

Typical Dish: Moroccan cuisine is as varied as its geography, climate, and people. However, most typical Moroccan dinners include a variety of cold or cooked salads and tajine. Tajine is both the name of a spicy stew and the clay pot where it is cooked. The pot has a domed lid that helps slowly cook meat to perfection. The tajine is served with flatbread called *khubz*. Couscous is a classic side dish served with *lben*, or buttermilk.

Food Etiquette: Knives are not necessary because meat is very tender. Tables are round to accommodate as many people as possible. Families gather around a main dish and share food. Moroccans usually use their right hand both to scoop up food with a piece of khubz and to make balls of couscous.

Drink Up! Moroccans drink mint tea throughout the day. It is steeped with fresh spearmint leaves. The strength of tea and how it is prepared vary from house to house and region to region.

Moroccans in Canada: Joseph Mimran was born in Casablanca, Morocco. He is a Canadian fashion designer best known for the Club Monaco and Joe Fresh lines of clothing.

Moroccan mint tea

> **"Everybody needs to keep in touch with their ancestors, and through food is one of the best ways to get close."**
>
> — Cornelia Walker Bailey, historian

GHANA

Typical Dish: Most Ghanaian dishes are made of rice, fufu or *banku* (corn dough), and a sauce or soup with fish, snails, other meat, or mushrooms. Groundnut soup made with peanuts (or peanut butter) is a specialty. *Waakye* (pronounced waa-chay) is a popular dish made with rice, beans, and dry sorghum leaves. It is usually served for breakfast or lunch. Many Ghanaian dishes require ingredients to be ground or pounded. This is done using a mortar and pestle or a grinding stone called an *asanka*.

Fufu served with palm nut soup and goat meat

Food Etiquette: In Ghana, food is often served from a big bowl for everyone at the table. People eat with no utensils. When using their hands to scoop food, people use the thumb and first two fingers of their right hand.

Drink Up! Among common beverages are *bissap* (iced tea made with dried hibiscus flowers) and *lamujee* (a spicy sweetened drink).

Ghanaians in Canada: The Ghanaian-Canadian Association of Saskatoon is an association for Ghanaians and friends of Ghana living and working in Saskatoon, Saskatchewan. One of its main objectives is to "preserve the unique culture, language, tradition, and heritage of Ghana."

FAVOURITE AFRICAN DESSERTS

CHAD: Millet cookies

Millet is a highly nutritious cereal. It has a mildly sweet flavour. Millet cookies are great snacks.

SENEGAL: Banana fritters

Sprinkle banana fritters with icing sugar or dip them in chocolate sauce. Eat them warm!

MADAGASCAR: *Koba akondro*

A batter made of mashed bananas, honey, and ground peanuts is steamed in a corn husk or banana leaf. After the packages cool down, this dessert is unwrapped and served.

Koba being sold by street vendors in Madagascar

MALI: *Dégué*

This dessert is made of sweetened couscous in a yogourt and milk base. It's best served chilled.

CONNECT IT

With a partner, choose one of the countries featured. What else would you like to know about this country's food traditions? After doing some additional research about the country's food traditions, tell a classmate what you find most interesting about what you found.

Chef VICTOR BONGO

READ THIS PROFILE of a Canadian chef who has turned traditional African food into a career he loves.

Chef Victor Bongo is famous in Vancouver's restaurant world. His culinary creations have been inspired by many cultures around the world. He has also been inspired by his mother's cooking. As a child, Bongo watched his mother cook his favourite foods, including rice, beans, and fried tilapia. These foods have become the inspiration for some of his award-winning recipes. One of his famous dishes is his flavourful African peanut soup.

Bongo was born in the Democratic Republic of the Congo (DRC). He grew up in Vancouver, British Columbia. While in high school, he met a teacher who saw his potential as a great chef and paid for him to go to cooking school.

Bongo took his unique cooking style to restaurants in Alberta and Yukon before returning to Vancouver. While in Yukon, he received the "Chef of the Year" award four years in a row, from 2008 to 2011. Bongo is also a writer. In 2009, he published a cookbook called *The Excellence of Chef Victor Bongo*. In 2015, he published a second cookbook, called *Chef Bongo from the Congo*.

Giving back to the community is as important to Bongo as cooking. He has worked with a children's hospital in Vancouver and opened an orphanage with more than 40 children in the DRC. He also works closely with the creators of *SuperChefs of the Universe*, a computer game focused on teaching children about healthy eating.

When asked about what inspires him, Bongo said: "To see youth showing interest in the food industry. Ten-year-old kids wanting to cook and teenagers doing culinary competitions."

culinary: *having to do with cooking*

Chef Bongo's famous African peanut soup

The Colours of Africa

Lillian O'Brien

THINK ABOUT IT

What do the clothes you wear say about you? Name three ideas someone might have about you based on the clothes you are wearing. Would all of these ideas be correct?

CLOTHING CAN SHOW off your personality. For some people, clothing can also be a connection to their ancestry and culture.

After Lillian O'Brien moved to Canada, she wanted to feel at home. She also wanted to spread her love for Africa and its many cultures. In this interview, O'Brien talks about how her African roots have helped her develop a clothing line, AfriCouture, and succeed in Canada.

NICOLE RICKETTS: Could you please describe your childhood in Zambia?

Lillian O'Brien: I had a different kind of childhood [from North American culture] when I was growing up. I didn't play with dolls for long as, by the age of four, my father realized that I had a head for math. My dad started showing me the ropes of working in his convenience stores and how to keep track of our sales and inventory. I loved working in the shops as that meant I didn't get to do all the other chores around the house with my sisters and brothers. It also guaranteed me a new bike all the time. My dad wanted to make sure I could cycle to the shops that were close by to go and take care of business. I loved the attention this brought me. As I grew older, I hated not being able to play with my siblings on Sundays as I had to work on more inventory.

NR: How did you come to make Canada your home?

LO: Canada became my home once I married a cowboy from Alberta! I met my husband, Jerry O'Brien, in Lusaka, Zambia, where he had been working for the Zambian Air Force. We got married in Harare, Zimbabwe, in 1996. In 2003, I came to Canada with my daughters to get some fresh air and to think about my life with my husband. Things changed very quickly in Zimbabwe once the president there announced [big changes]. I decided to stay in Canada because my daughters were very happy here. I flew back and forth from Vancouver to Harare for about three years. By 2006, it became clear I could no longer manage to run my [fashion] business there. So I made the decision to pack up and ship a few memorabilia to Vancouver and apply for residency here.

Model wearing an O'Brien creation at Vancouver Fashion Week in 2007

38

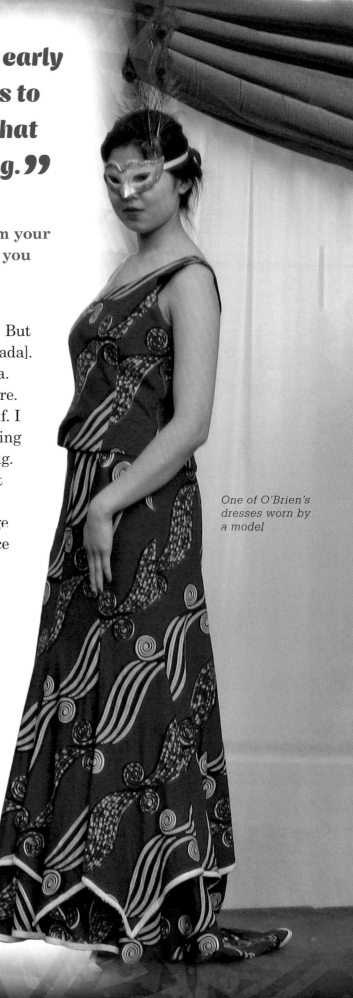

▼▼▼▼▼▼▼▼▼▼▼▼▼▼▼▼▼▼▼▼▼

66 One of the things I learnt early on as a fashion designer is to always strive to design what everyone else is not making. 99

▲▲▲▲▲▲▲▲▲▲▲▲▲▲▲▲▲▲▲▲▲

NR: How did your skills and experience from your career as a fashion designer in Zambia help you establish your business in Canada?

LO: One would think after being in the fashion industry for more than 25 years, it would be easy. But it has been very challenging to start over [in Canada]. First of all, I had become "Lady O'Brien" in Africa. Many people did all the everyday work for me there. But here in Canada, I had to do everything myself. I didn't even remember when I had last used a sewing machine — let alone spent hours making anything. However, I realized that … I could definitely start over and learn how to do things myself. The designing and sewing was the easy part. The huge challenge came when I needed financial assistance to set up my business. As a new immigrant, that was very hard. Sometimes I would tell myself, "Better move back to Africa, where I don't have to introduce myself twice." But I have learnt that anything that is worth doing requires patience, resilience, and determination. I have opened up shops more times than I care to count, simply because I will not give up.

One of the things I learnt early on as a fashion designer is to always strive to design what everyone else is not making. I am my own biggest fan and model. I love to be different and stand out in a crowd wherever I go, and the women that come to me for clothes expect nothing less.

One of O'Brien's dresses worn by a model

resilience: *ability to recover quickly from difficulties*

NR: You once said: "My clothing line is influenced very much by my African background, but has to be very much a Canadian product." Why do you think it is important to blend both styles?

LO: AfriCouture celebrates the bold and vibrant colours of Africa but with a Western flair. AfriCouture has to reflect our Canadian lifestyle, as that is how we can get everyone curious and fascinated enough to want to wear our sometimes very bold colours. AfriCouture clothing also has to be made in such a way that it can fit into the busy Canadian way of life and comfortable enough to wear to work.

▼▼▼▼▼▼▼▼▼▼▼▼▼▼▼▼▼▼▼▼▼

> ❝ AfriCouture celebrates the bold and vibrant colours of Africa but with a western flair. ❞

▲▲▲▲▲▲▲▲▲▲▲▲▲▲▲▲▲▲▲▲▲

AfriCouture also highlights the difference in the cultures and traditions across the African continent. The clothes are designed and made from African fabrics. Fabrics are dyed and woven very differently in most African countries. It is wonderful to share the knowledge of how the fabrics are made and on what occasion they are used.

NR: African fabrics have floral patterns and prints in bright colours. How do these fabrics reflect your personality?

LO: African prints are very floral and very bright, and they totally reflect my personality. I always want to look happy and bright — even in the winter. Most people will immediately start a conversation with me because I look bright and cheerful! Who wouldn't love to put a smile on a face wherever they went?

flair: *style and originality*

Models line up during O'Brien's fashion show.

NR: How do you think that keeping your homeland traditions and culture alive have helped you in Canada?

LO: … My African culture has helped me get noticed as "the new kid on block" because I dared to be different. If I hadn't, I would be just another new immigrant.

I continue to be African. It is up to us to keep our cultures alive and relevant by sharing them with our fellow Canadians and those in our community. Our children will only continue this conversation if we show them how proud we are about our culture and traditions. When my daughter got married in June 2014, the first thing I did when it was my turn to speak was pay homage to our ancestors and other family members who have passed away. This is how we start celebrations and also seek their blessing. I did that because I am not embarrassed to share my culture and traditions with my friends and acquaintances.

NR: Do you miss life in Zambia or Zimbabwe at all? If you do, what do you miss most?

LO: I miss Zambia and Zimbabwe all the time. I often think of the life we enjoyed back home and how things were so much easier with the help [I had] and seamstresses to do all my sewing. I miss the family barbecue over the weekends and how people there are always ready to help when in need. I miss living in those huge homes and spending hours under the thatched gazebo sipping some wine while watching my daughters play in the swimming pool. I miss those African moonlights that brighten up the entire space as though the sun is out.

I will always treasure that part of my life, but I will build new traditions here in Canada and create a new culture. Life is what we make of it, and I will make sure that my grandchildren live a great life here in Canada so that we can make new memories. We will have the best of both worlds!

Model wearing an O'Brien creation

CONNECT IT

Look up the meaning of the Sankofa symbol of the Akan people of West Africa. How could you use the Sankofa symbol on a piece of fabric, clothing, or a piece of art? Tell a classmate why you think the Sankofa symbol is important.

Himba women in northern Namibia braid and cover their hair with a mixture of ground ochre and butter.

ALL ABOUT HAIR

THINK ABOUT IT

List three things that make you unique. For example, you could include your hairstyle, a special talent, or an unusual hobby.

IN AFRICAN CULTURES, hair is more than just stylish. It may show age, religion, clan membership, rank, or marital status. For example, girls from Senegal shave their heads to show that they are not ready for marriage. Young men in Kenya get elaborate hairstyles to show they have completed the rites needed to become adults.

Traditionally, hairdressing is carried out by friends or relatives. However, in Senegal and Ghana, hairdressing can be carried out only by members of the same sex. After cleaning, oiling, and brushing, the hair may be styled into braids, curls, or twists. Some flowers, beads, or other objects may be added, too.

TYPES OF BRAIDS

Bantu knots are a series of twisted knots on top of the head.

Cornrows are braided in straight lines that are very close to the head. They are sometimes called canerows or just rows. Like some other styles of braids, cornrows can be decorated with beads or shells.

Senegalese twists look like ropes. They are also known as rope twists. They can be done with natural hair or with hair extensions.

Mohawks come in many variations. In general, the sides of the head have shorter hair than the middle. The sides of the head can either be shaved or in tight braids or dreadlocks. The hair in the middle can be spiked, coloured, or dreadlocked.

Nubian twists look like tight springs. The twists are soft and light. It is a comfortable style for today's fashionistas.

Eritrean braids look like cornrows. However, the ends of the hair are not braided, leaving long strands of hair.

CONNECT IT

Braiding is a tradition passed on from generation to generation. Think of a tradition in your own life that has been passed on from another generation. Why is it important to you?

South Africa's
PAINTED HOUSES

THINK ABOUT IT

Why do you think it is important that elders pass their knowledge on to younger generations?

THE NDEBELE WOMEN of South Africa have a colourful tradition. They decorate the walls of their houses with bright patterns. This tradition shows their artistic skills. It lets them express their culture. This tradition is passed down from generation to generation. Read this Q&A to learn more about how Ndebele house painting is staying alive.

Artist Francina Mbonani coming out of her house, Mabhoko village, Africa

Ndebele children learn how to paint traditional Ndebele patterns.

Who are the Ndebele?

The Ndebele are a group of people who live in South Africa. At the end of the 19th century, the Ndebele and the Boers (White people in South Africa) went to war. The Ndebele people lost the war and their lives became very difficult. The Ndebele people expressed their grief and worry through art. They created their own tradition and style of house painting. This tradition united them as a group.

Do all Ndebele people paint houses?

Only Ndebele women paint houses. They transfer designs and colours from their beadwork to wall painting. Women express their identity as individuals and as part of a group through their art.

Ndebele women pass their skills from mother to daughter. Young girls withdraw from male society for three months and are taught the art of beading and wall painting. They are taught how to mix paint, how to apply it, and the basics of symmetry and geometric design.

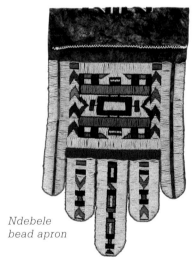
Ndebele bead apron

◀ Ndebele women are widely known for their glass beadwork. Their beadwork traditions go back hundreds of years. Women apply colourful beads to their bridal aprons, necklaces, and costumes.

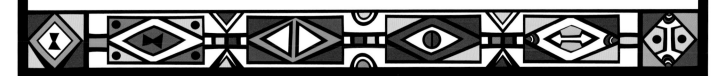

Francina Ndimande inside her house

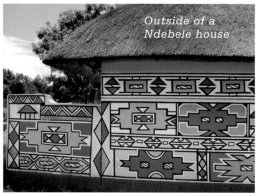

Outside of a Ndebele house

The village church

What do the women paint on the walls?

The images that were first painted on walls came from beadwork patterns. Women painted geometric patterns with only earth tones and white paint.

Over time, women incorporated new colours and patterns. Motifs now include objects such as light bulbs, razor blades, swimming pools, telephones, and faucets. These are objects the Ndebele know of but may not be able to afford.

In times of war, paintings were used to pass on political messages, show family lineage, or mark territorial boundaries. The paintings became signposts for other people to recognize the houses as Ndebele houses. The oppressors viewed this cultural form as decorative and harmless. Today, some paintings honour ancestors and serve as prayers. Other paintings depict a time in a woman's life or her emotions.

What painting techniques are used?

Painting is done freehand. The women use no rulers. Designs are planned in advance, but they aren't sketched out. Artwork is done mostly on the house exteriors. However, some artists decorate the inside walls as well.

When painting, the artist divides the wall into sections with diagonal lines. Next, she paints the black outline of the design. Then, she fills in the black outlines with colour. The final step is to touch up the black outlines.

In the past, paints came only from nature. Brown, red, and ochre shades came from clay and earth. White and black came from lime and coal. The walls had to be repainted frequently because the rain washed away the paint. Today, Ndebele women still use natural pigments, but sometimes include acrylic paints as well. This helps paintings last longer. Artists use their fingers and chicken feathers as paintbrushes.

Motifs: *decorative images or designs*
lineage: *past members of a family; ancestry*
oppressors: *people who abuse or treat others harshly*